THE PILGRIMS OF PLIMOTH

written and illustrated by Marcia Sewall

Aladdin Paperbacks

The quotes on pp. 6, 7, 8, 10, 11, 12, 14, 19, 46 are taken from:
OF PLYMOUTH PLANTATION 1620–1647 by William Bradford

The quotes on pp. 10, 26 are taken from:
A JOURNAL OF THE PILGRIMS AT PLYMOUTH generally called "Mourt's Relation,"
originally printed in 1622

The quotes on pp. 14, 16, 36, 44 are taken from the words of the present-day Pilgrim Village Interpreters

First Aladdin Paperbacks edition September 1996

Aladdin Paperbacks
An imprint of Simon & Schuster
Children's Publishing Division
1230 Avenue of the Americas
New York, NY 10020

Also available in an Atheneum Books for Young Readers edition

Manufactured in China

22 24 26 28 30 29 27 25 23

The Library of Congress has cataloged the hardcover edition as follows:

Sewall, Marcia.   The pilgrims of Plimoth.

SUMMARY: Chronicles, in text and illustrations, the
day-to-day life of the early Pilgrims
in the Plimoth Colony.
1. Pilgrims (New Plymouth colony)—Juvenile literature.   2. Massachusetts—Social life and
customs—Colonial period, ca. 1600–1775—Juvenile literature.   [1. Pilgrims (New Plymouth colony)
2. Massachusetts—Social life and customs—Colonial period, ca. 1600–1775]   I. Title.
F68.S49   1986   974.4'82   86-3362
ISBN 978-0-689-31250-2 (hardcover)
ISBN 978-0-689-80861-6 (Aladdin pbk.)
1019 SCP

This book is dedicated to The Pilgrim Village Interpreters,
whose great spirit gives life to our Plimoth pilgrims.

———————————————

I wish to thank Patty Wolcott Berger, Caroline Chapin
of the Pilgrim Society, and Len Travers
of Plimoth Plantation, especially.

THE PILGRIMS

Aye, Governor Bradford calls us pilgrims. We are English and England was our home. We left behind us much that we loved when we came to America. But our lives were ruled by King James and for many years it seemed as though our very hearts were in prison in England. We believe it is the Bible, only, that can instruct us in the ways of the Lord. We have to worship freely.

September, 1620, our lives changed. We were seventy menfolk and womenfolk, thirty-two good children, a handful of cocks and hens, and two dogs, gathered together on a dock in Plymouth, England, ready to set sail for America in a small ship called the *Mayflower*. It is true that among us were, and are, people who are not pilgrims and we call them "strangers," though the name displeases them some. They came to America, not to form a Godly community, but to gain wealth. Our trip was costly, but English merchants loaned us money, hoping to prosper in time by our successful settlement.

After an abundance of prayers and tears we made farewells at dockside and boarded our small ship. Our voyage across the Atlantic Ocean "began with a prosperous wind," but the sea soon became "sharp and violent" and storms howled about us. Water washed across and down through our decks and almost took John Howland overboard. A baby was born, Oceanus Hopkins he was named. November 12th, a Sabbath Day, we arrived in America. We praised God for our safe journey and this new land.

We intended to form our plantation "some place about Hudson's River," in the territory of Northern Virginia, but we were off course and weary with our voyage. It is grateful we were to reach any land safely, and thus we came to New England, first landing on the point of Cape Cod. While still on board ship, in preparation for life in America, we agreed upon laws of behavior. The freemen signed their names to this document and we elected John Carver our governor.

We took the shallop, our small sailing vessel, ashore to be repaired by the *Mayflower*'s carpenter. Its sides had sprung and its seams needed caulking, but it had served well as sleeping quarters on our voyage. Some of the menfolk, laden with armor, rowed to shore in the ship's long boat to explore, and womenfolk bundled up laundry and went ashore, too, for a morning of washing. Indeed, they washed with pleasure on that Monday after being overmany days at sea!

But it seemed as though the land offered nothing. It was a "hideous and desolate wilderness, full of wild beasts and wild men." Aye, but it did give to us one great gift: a strange Indian seed of many colors stored in baskets under mounds of earth. Corn seed! We desperately needed that corn seed and we took it. Later we would pay the Indians for our "gift." And wanting to remember that place forever, we named it Cornhill. From thence, too, we took back juniper which we burnt on shipboard to ease the now stinking smell. After days on shore, the men returned to find a healthy new baby aboard the *Mayflower*. Mistress White had given birth to a boy-child to be named Peregrine White. God be praised!

Down the bay-side of the cape some of our brave men sailed in the now fit shallop, looking for a safe and deep harbor for our ship and a place to "pitch our dwellings." Plimoth seemed a goodly place, so the *Mayflower* followed. December 16th, winter was upon us. Looking a-land we saw scrub trees and great trees growing down to "the brink of the sea," and on the hills there were large cornfields stubbly with age. And by God's grace, when we explored we found "a very sweet brook" and plentiful springs nearby. And no Indian "greeted" us! Our good fortune increased

for in the woods were wild fowl, hare and deer, nuts and berries, and the sea was abundant with fish (but our hooks were too large for catching them). The sassafras tree, with root bark so valued in England as medicine, grew here also. Though ill and exhausted, we were ready to begin our lives at New Plimoth in this "strange and hard land." We set to work. December 22nd, a deadborn son was delivered by goodwife Allerton.

On Christmas day we started building the Common House for the benefit of all. Some men cut and felled trees, others carried them to the clearing and those who were skilled rived and sawed logs, shaping them for building purposes. The young folk scouted the shore for roof thatch reeds. It was very hard work. And now there was sickness about. Our Common House turned into the likes of a hospital and we took care of each other. Those still well enough struggled to put up dwelling houses and shelters, but the ground was frozen and our hands and feet were bitter cold. Here in America there were "no friends to welcome (us) nor inns to entertain or refresh (our) weatherbeaten bodies," which became even weaker with coughs and fever. The General Sickness was upon us.

Half of our community died that first winter, including our
Governor, John Carver, and little Oceanus Hopkins born on the *May-
flower.* But "the Lord giveth and the Lord taketh according to his will."
With great sadness we buried our dead on a hill overlooking the harbor.
Of the survivors, scarce fifty in number, over half were children. We

elected William Bradford our new Governor and looked ahead. In April the *Mayflower* returned to England with only the crew. Though we could have sailed home, we chose to remain in America. It was a frightening beginning, but it was God's will.

MENFOLK

We rise each day as the sun comes up. With haste we stir up the coals and get the fire burning. We are glad to know the warmth of a fire on this cold morning. Feel the bread and such, frozen and only four feet from the hearth. Last night you may be sure we slept deep beneath the bed rugs! And today it is layers of clothes we will be wearing. Our rough linen shirt is worn night and day and we are fast to put on woolen socks and shoes before walking upon the cold earthen floor. Quickly we climb into our breeches, a warm doublet, and today, a leather jerkin. If it is many miles we will be walking, well, then we'll place sprigs of mugwort plant in our shoes to ease the journey. Before we break the fast we ask the Lord, "Please give us strength to do your will and to know your word." If we are well and able, we will go about our humble duties, foul weather or fair. No man rests. It is at noon that we will return home for a large meal, again to give thanks.

Aye, some of us menfolk have an English grammar school educa-
tion and a few men, like Elder Brewster, are college educated. But we must
be fishermen and farmers here. Our hands are as important as our heads
if we would survive. We work hard to tame this wilderness of ours. We cut

back woods to expose fields to sun and rain. That first spring, without horse or plow, we cleared twenty acres of land. We planted mounds of Indian corn and bushels of barley and peas. At harvest time, "instead of famine, God gave (us) plenty."

For safety we built our houses close together with a broad street betwixt them. Each small house is sided with wide boards or narrow clapboards; our floors are oft-times made of wood, but also made of bare earth soaked with water and flattened smooth. Our rooms with wooden walls are dark, save the light of the fire. But sometimes, in building our houses, we fill the space betwixt the heavy upright posts with wattle sticks, or laths, smeared with daub and whitened with lime. That white against the darkness pleases us and reminds us of our English homes. Our chimneys are made in the same fashion. Our roofs are shingled or thatched with sun-dried reeds. A gentle light filters in through our few small windows covered with linen soaked in linseed oil, a light that softens the harshness of our lives. And in the warmth of spring and summer we slide those windows open and in come shafts of sunlight and those pesky mosquitoes! Governor Bradford says, "You'd better stay in England until you become mosquito proof!" But for many months it seems as though our most constant light comes from the fire on our hearth.

It is our responsibility to make decisions and laws. What shall be the punishment for idle gossip? Shall a man be placed in the stocks for gaming on Sunday? And what about Goody Billington? Why, she was seen about the plantation after dark, when the vapours are most foul and none but thieves would dare be out, save for the ward keeping watch over us from high upon the fort. Aye, we have a constable here and several magistrates who maintain laws, but we are mainly law-abiding people.

And it is our responsibility to protect our women and children from Spanish and French and Indian attack. Indeed, Capt. Miles Standish has trained each man to bear a firing piece and he leads us in musket drills. We have impaled our community round with a palisade fence. It keeps safe our busy village from the vast unknown that surrounds our lives.

How we feared those unclothed and painted savages when we first came to America. Indians are so unlike Englishmen! They move about the woods as specks of light and shadow. They are as silent as snow. No loud conversation or clanking armor or musket fire can be heard from them, just an arrow from nowhere! In March of our first year of settlement, a tall sagamore named Samoset surprised us with a friendly visit. He told us that his tribe came not from here. That the Indians hereabouts were called Patuxets, but a deadly plague had destroyed them four years before our arrival. All but one, named Squanto, who was elsewhere in the world as a captive of Englishmen.

Squanto became our helpful friend. Aye, our language he knew and so could interpret for us Indian affairs. He was the pilot of our shallop as we explored the coast of America. He understood the ways of nature and taught us to plant corn when the oak bud had burst and the leaves were as big as a mouse's ear. He taught us how to catch herring and how to fertilize our harsh soil with them when we planted corn seed. He taught us to tread eels out of the river mud in warm seasons and to catch them by hand. And he taught us how to catch them through winter's ice.

Samoset also introduced us to a great sachem of these parts named Massasoit. And in our first year of settlement we made a peace treaty with him. We agreed that his people must not hurt our people, or bear punishment; we agreed not to steal from each other; and to leave our weapons behind when we came to each other upon any occasion; and we agreed to help each other if we should suffer attack. Aye, we have respected and honored that treaty. Now we walk "as peacefully and

safely in the woods as in the highways of England."

Our first wondrous harvest called for celebration. We sang psalms and played games. We rejoiced and fired our noisy muskets into the air. And the Indians came and joined in the feasting; not just an Indian or two, but Massasoit arrived with over ninety braves who stayed among us for three festive days. We prayed and gave thanks for such a harvest and our survival.

WOMENFOLK

Our days are full. We take our little ones into the fields when we must help with the harvest, but we are needed most at our hearths and near our homes. Our men return hungry from woods and fields at the noon hour and our many children are never full. But "children are a gift from God and we favor all the small folk the good Lord's got to send us." Mornings we spend in preparation of the midday meal; bread baked, a pottage made or the roasting meat needs turning on the spit. And our homes need care. As many as nine (and more, if need be) share this simple house and they are not all of a family at that. On occasion there is a shipwrecked sailor needs lodging or there are new folks to the plantation in need of a roof. And in this house we have an indentured servant who, for food and shelter, works. Our furnishings are few. Our table is naught but a board set betwixt two barrels. We stand or sit much informal about the room to eat. Our plate is a trencher of wood or of pewter; our most useful utensils are our hands, though we do use spoons. Aye, and we enjoy large napkins!

What belongings we have shipped with us to America. Though a fine bedstead is a sign of wealth, most of our beds are but a straw or feather mattress laid out upon the floor. A cradle sets by the hearth for warmth; there is a chair for the good husband, a trunk, a cupboard, a settle or stool or two about the room. The fireplace, however, is well-furnished with andirons and lug pole; pot-hooks and trammels; and spits and kettles. Nearby are pipkins and pottles for all purposes. Our rooms are fragrant with the smell of clothes and food, people and herbs, straw and earth and the ever-present smell of a fire burning on the hearth.

During the warming months of spring and during those glorious summer and fall months we rise with the first light and work till sundown preparing for winter. The root crops must be gathered and stored, fish gutted and packed in salt. Fruits must be pickled and preserved, including cow cumber pickles, the favorites of our children; pompions must be cut into pieces, strung and hung from the rafters to dry, along with onions and corn, and herbs for medicine and seasoning; there, too, hang pretty marigolds to color our butter, to flavor our food, and strengthen our hearts. In fall our swine must be slaughtered, scalded, scraped and cured. And fat must be rendered into soap.

We do not have overmany clothes and we work hard to keep what well-worn garments we have patched and mended. We have neither spinning wheels nor looms here. Our clothes are mostly English-made. But during those tedious, long winter months when there is a bit of time to spare, we will sit about the fire and sew a jerkin for our husbands or knit a new pair of stockings for the children. And in summer, when there is evening light about, we will make a pair of sleeves for ourselves or add a ruffle to a petticoat. To freshen up a bodice or a skirt we will dye it in a bath of tansy or woad, iris or goldenrod and hang it over the fence to dry. We are grateful for God's gifts.

The sick need nursing and the young need care. How often we are called upon to brew an infusion or a decoction of herbs or to administer a poultice. But for a great illness we will call upon Surgeon Fuller. It is he who pulls teeth and leeches us spring and fall. We seldom bathe, for removing our clothes would expose our bodies to foul vapours. As the sun sets we are grateful for rest. God protect and preserve us.

CHILDREN AND YOUNGFOLK

Nay, we have neither school nor schoolmaster here, but our elders hope for a schoolmaster soon to come from England. We learn obedience from our parents and if we are naughty we are told to "go mend our manners or we will get a proper thump on the britch!" It is our father who will find himself before the village magistrate and, indeed, in the stocks if he will not look to our behavior. Then all the village shall pass by and stare at him and make dreadful comment.

At dawn we take buckets and run to fetch water from the village spring. The grass is damp and the cobwebs sparkle in the early morning light of summer. The air smells of salt from the ocean. And we must also fetch wood for the hearth fire. After breaking the fast on bread, forced eggs and little beer we begin to work. We will feed scratch to the hens, milk the cows and goats and take them to the meadow to graze, and on the way home we will stop to pick sky-blue whortleberries. In the fall we will drive our swine to the oak woods to feed on acorn and other ground nuts. And there are days when we must muck out the animal pens.

In early spring we will help poke seeds into the freshly worked earth and then spend hours stoning crows away from those seeds. And as the seeds sprout, we must pull the unwanted tares from the garden. But we don't mind spending time in the garden for we know what it is like to have no food. We know how it feels to be cold and hungry. We remember our first winter in America. At harvest time, in late summer, we pick Indian corn and peas and beans. We gather in wheat and rye and barley and crabapples for vergi. If we are strong, we will gather thatch for

roofing and wattle for walls. We learn to shape wood for fences, for clapboards, for spoons and bowls and tubs and troughs and such.

When there has been much rain and sun throughout the growing season and the harvest is wondrous fair, we may celebrate with games and feasting. We play "hide and seek" and sometimes hide under a pile of sweet hay in the cowshed. We play "blindman's bluff" and "stool ball." We play "pitch the bar" and "tug o'war." And we love to footrace down the broad street of our village.

We that are the young misses here learn of housewifery. We learn to grind corn and barley and wheat. We learn to feel the weight of a measure of flour in our hands, to sift flour through a boulter of cloth; to know a pinch of salt and a dash of mace; to scour and scald; to bruise; to sleep a pottage and to broach a piece of meat. We learn to judge a warm and a hot fire. We learn to knead the soft dough with the heels of our hands, to rise it and form it into lovely round loaves of cheate bread. We learn how to bake in the outdoor oven. And there we hear the news of our elders.

Boxed into small garden patches beside our houses are herbs. Their many uses are taught to us by our mothers. There are pot herbs like spinage and violet leaves, red sage and mint which we put into sallats. There are root herbs like carrots and turnips and jerusalem artichokes which are delicious in a pottage. And there are herbs to ease sickness. A decoction of mullein is good for a toothache and the leaves are good for the cough of the lungs of a cow. A poultice of onion will heal the bite of a mad dog. And an infusion of thyme, taken at bedtime, will keep away nightmares. We learn to strew rosemary in the room for cleansing the bad airs when sickness is about, and rue to keep away pesky flies; we use soapwort for scouring bowls and the biting smell of southernwood to discourage moths.

We learn to spin wool on a hand spindle and to knit. We learn to cross-stitch and feather-stitch, blind-stitch and back-stitch. We begin our first sampler and soon will help with the mending and making of clothes.

Betwixt sundown Saturday and sunset Sunday is the Lord's Day. For many hours we sit in the large room beneath the fort to worship. "It matters not where we worship for we know that it is the people who are the church." And at times we watch the hourglass slowly trickle sand. We listen to our elders read from the Bible. We listen to Governor Bradford give sermon. We try to hear and be instructed in the ways of the Lord. Our fathers must not work in the fields nor fish nor hunt on the Sabbath. Our mothers must not bake nor work about the hearth on the Sabbath. And we must not play. The Sabbath is the Lord's Day and we give thanks.

THE PLANTATION

With most of our Indian neighbors we are at peace. And with them we trade our cloth, and iron pots and pans, and farming tools for their animal skins, especially that of the beaver. We ship those skins to English merchants who turn them into fancy coats and hats for sale in England. We also ship clapboards and soft woods which they have little of in England, and fish, and sassafras. Thus we pay off our debt and we begin to prosper.

Here in America the air is good and the water is wholesome. We "feel the sweetness of the country." Our health is restored. More ships arrive with more passengers and our plantation begins to grow. Ten years have passed since we came to America. We now have bulls and cows and calfs to sell. Our fields extend into the wilderness. People from Plimoth colony are beginning to move outside the plantation for want of more land and are settling in Duxbarow and other diverse townships. And there is a new, fast growing colony at the head of Massachusetts Bay. Long have we struggled to survive. Now we prosper. Our greatest wealth is our harvest, our healthy families and a place to worship freely. God be praised.

GLOSSARY

BOULTER – a sifter

BREECHES – trousers slightly below knee-length

BROACH – to put on a spit for cooking purposes

CHEATE BREAD – good bread, but not the finest

COW CUMBER PICKLES – cucumber pickles

DAUB – plaster made from clay, sand, sheep's dung, straw, and water

DECOCTION – a liquid solution made by boiling down ingredients

DOUBLET – jacket of cloth or leather, usually with sleeves and open down the front

FORCED EGGS – scrambled eggs

INFUSION – a liquid solution made by steeping ingredients, then straining them

JERKIN – jacket of cloth or leather, open at the neck, often without sleeves

JUNIPER – an aromatic evergreen plant

LEECHES – used in bleeding a patient, believed to balance the body fluids.

LITTLE BEER – light beer which was drunk in England instead of the polluted water

LUG POLE – a long pole the width of a chimney, made of green wood or iron, from which hung pots and kettles

MUGWORT – a plant believed to have magical properties

PIPKINS – saucepans of various shapes and sizes

POMPIONS – pumpkins

POT-HOOKS & TRAMMELS – devices that hang from the lug pole and support pots and kettles

POTTAGE – stew

POTTLES – two-quart jugs

POULTICE – moist mass applied to inflamed part of the body

SACHEM – the chief of an Indian tribe

SAGAMORE – a minor Algonquin Indian chief

SALLATS – salads

SAMPLER – a piece of cloth embroidered with different stitches

SETTLE – a long bench made with a high back for blocking drafts

SPINAGE – spinach

SPIT – a long rod to stick through a piece of meat for cooking purposes

TANSY – a common plant with yellow flowers

TARES – weeds

TRENCHER – a piece of wood, hollowed out some, for holding food

VERGI – vinegar

WARD – night watch

WATTLE – rods and twigs, to be woven together and used in building

WHORTLEBERRIES – blueberries

WOAD – an herb grown for the blue dyestuff yielded by its leaves